The Disappearance of Maura Murray

A Chilling True Crime Investigation Into the New Hampshire Cold Case That Still Defies Answers

Richie J. Garst

**Copyright © 2025 by Richie J. Garst.
All rights reserved.**

No part of this book may be copied, stored, or transmitted in any form or by any means, electronic or mechanical, including photocopying and recording, without prior written permission from the author, except for brief quotations in reviews or critical articles.

This book is a work of nonfiction. Some names and identifying details may have been changed to protect the privacy of individuals.

DISCLAIMER

This book is a work of nonfiction based on real events. Every effort has been made to present information accurately and fairly, drawing from publicly available sources, historical records, and documented accounts.

The author does not claim to provide new evidence or investigative findings. While care has been taken to ensure accuracy, some details may be subject to differing interpretations. Names, identifying details, or minor circumstances may have been changed to protect the privacy of individuals.

This book is intended for informational and educational purposes only. It is not meant to sensationalize tragedy, interfere with ongoing investigations, or cause harm to victims, their families, or communities. The author and publisher disclaim any liability for how the information is used or interpreted by readers.

ACKNOWLEDGEMENTS

I would like to extend my sincere gratitude to the researchers, journalists, and dedicated individuals who have worked tirelessly to keep Maura Murray's case in the public eye. Their commitment to uncovering truth and preserving accuracy has provided the foundation upon which this book rests.

To Maura's family, who continue to carry the weight of unanswered questions with strength and dignity—this work is written with respect for your journey and in recognition of your enduring courage.

Finally, to the readers: thank you for engaging with this story not only as a mystery, but as a human tragedy. By seeking understanding, you play a part in ensuring that Maura, and others like her, are never forgotten.

DEDICATION

For Maura Murray—
A life full of promise, a story left unfinished, and a name that continues to echo through time.

And for every family still searching for answers—
May hope, truth, and justice never fade.

CONTENTS

PROLOGUE 8
    The Vanishing Moment 8

CHAPTER 1 13
    A Life in Context 13

CHAPTER 2 19
    The Day of Disappearance 19

CHAPTER 3 25
    The Accident on Route 112 25

CHAPTER 4 30
    Friends, Family, and the Alarm 30

CHAPTER 5 35
    The Investigation Begins 35

CHAPTER 6 41
    Theories Emerge 41

CHAPTER 7 49
    Suspects and Leads 49

CHAPTER 8 57
    Online Sleuths and Public Obsession 57

CHAPTER 9... **64**
    Long-Term Investigations...64

CHAPTER 10... **71**
    Theories, Controversies, and Legacy......................71

EPILOGUE... **77**
    Vanished but Not Forgotten.....................................77

CLOSING SECTION... **81**
    Key Lessons Learned..81
    Modern Safety Strategies....................................... 83
    Inside the Criminal Mind... 85
    Honoring the Victims...87
    Extended Resources.. 88

Author's Note

Writing about Maura Murray's disappearance has been both a responsibility and a journey. This book is not meant to sensationalize her story but to preserve it with care, accuracy, and respect. Maura was more than a headline or a case file—she was a daughter, a sister, and a friend whose life continues to matter.

In assembling this work, I have drawn from verified reports, public records, and credible sources. While questions remain unanswered, I have sought to present the facts clearly, explore the theories thoughtfully, and honor the enduring human impact of this case.

True crime is not entertainment—it is the lived reality of real people. My hope is that this book deepens awareness, encourages reflection, and keeps the memory of Maura alive while reminding us all of the importance of compassion, vigilance, and truth.

To her family, friends, and to those still searching for answers: this book is dedicated to you.

PROLOGUE

The Vanishing Moment

The air was biting cold that February night in 2004, the type of cold that makes quiet sharper and the darkness heavier. Route 112 near Haverhill, New Hampshire, was vacant save for the infrequent headlights that swept across areas of snow and ice. Around 7:30 p.m., a car sat tilted off the tiny rural road, its nose slanted toward a small embankment. The Saturn sedan's front end was damaged, and a spiderweb fracture spread across the glass.

To passing automobiles, the incident seemed like just another winter collision. But when they slowed, something seemed odd. The road was slick but not dangerous enough to explain the location of the automobile. And more unnerving was the lack of its driver.

One of the first people to observe the crash moved his vehicle to the side and gazed at the Saturn. The headlights were still on, throwing a pale yellow glow against the snow. Inside, the airbags had deployed, and the inside appeared curiously unkempt. A carton of wine sat on the back seat, some of it dripping over the upholstery.

Moments later, a school bus driver who lived nearby got home and, noticing the automobile from his window, went to check on it. He moved up to the car and spotted a young lady moving near the driver's seat. She appeared dazed, maybe hurt.

"Do you need me to call someone?" he asked softly, trying not to shock her.

The lady shook her head swiftly. "No, I've already called AAA. My pals are on the way."

Her voice was calm but short, as if she wanted the talk finished before it started. The bus driver looked back at the automobile, then at the silent, deserted road. Something about her statements didn't sit right. This segment of Route 112 has minimal to no mobile reception. He knew since he drove it regularly.

"You're sure you're all set?" He asked again.

"Yes," she answered forcefully, eyes darting down. "I don't need help."

The guy paused, then moved aside, reassured enough to leave her alone. But within minutes, when police arrived at the site after another driver made a 911 call, the Saturn was empty. No vehicle, no tracks heading away from the snow-packed shoulder—just quiet.

The responding officer swept his flashlight around the area. The beam remained on the mangled automobile, the gushing wine, and the glaring absence of its passenger.

Where has the young lady gone?

To comprehend that night, detectives started retracing Maura Murray's movements in the last hours before her abduction.

Earlier in the day, Maura had contacted her college instructors, informing them she would be absent due to a family situation. She gathered everything from her dorm room, including textbooks and clothes, and arranged them neatly in her vehicle. To friends and teachers, nothing appeared too frightening. But the subtle, purposeful elements subsequently become jigsaw pieces in a broader enigma.

Around 4 p.m., she took $280 from an ATM in Amherst, Massachusetts. Surveillance video showed a woman standing alone at the machine, face inscrutable, before sliding the cash into her wallet. She then stopped at a local liquor shop, acquiring boxed wine and many bottles of alcoholic booze. The receipt timestamp was added to the timeline.

By early evening, she was on the road, heading north across the darkening winter countryside. Highway cameras showed her Saturn moving away from campus. Phone records revealed a call to check her voicemail, but otherwise no outbound calls were made.

The trek north had no obvious objective. The family would subsequently swear there had been no emergency, no crisis needing her to depart. Yet she traveled hours into New Hampshire, aiming for the White Mountains, an area she had once visited with her father.

The automobile crash on Route 112 was the final verified sighting. Locals reported her as being bewildered but not gravely hurt. The bus driver's statement was consistent: she said she didn't require support. Minutes later, she was gone.

The road was too silent, the snow too exposing, and the chronology too thin for explanations. If Maura had gone away, where were her tracks? If someone picked her up, who would take this secluded road on a chilly Monday night?

Her life had already been in motion toward some concealed conclusion. Now, at this motionless roadside sight, the inquiry sank into quiet.

What caused Maura Murray to leave her vehicle behind and flee into the New Hampshire night?

CHAPTER 1

A Life in Context

The Murray family was huge, close-knit, and Irish Catholic. Raised in Hanson, Massachusetts, Maura was the fourth of five children in a home that balanced affection, discipline, and perseverance. Her father, Fred Murray, worked hard to provide stability, and her mother, Laurie, was recognized for her strength and love for her children.

Maura grew up in the shadow of elder siblings who excelled in school and athletics. Her sister Julie, in particular, had already blazed a road at the U.S. Military Academy at West Point, establishing a high standard for performance. Maura followed her route, entering West Point herself before transferring to the University of Massachusetts Amherst to study nursing.

Teachers described her as clever but quiet, a young lady who absorbed material rapidly and pushed herself more than others. On the track, she exhibited the same dedication. Running large distances appeared to reflect her personality: steady, enduring, and concentrated.

Her friends remembered a different side—the one who laughed readily, who could flip from seriousness to playful mocking in an instant. She was faithful, typically the person friends confided in. Yet, they occasionally observed an undercurrent of passion that distinguished her as unique. She wanted to perform well, to achieve, and to avoid disappointing people around her.

One previous coach characterized her this way:

"She wasn't the loudest on the team, but she was reliable. You could rely on her to show up, to put in the effort, and to finish strong. She carried herself like she had something to prove—but in a calm, resolute way."

At West Point, Maura originally looked to flourish. She donned the uniform with pride, appreciating the disciplined atmosphere. But within a short time, fissures formed. The rigorous obligations of military life conflicted with her personal desires. Transferring to UMass seemed like a release, a chance to concentrate on nursing, a job that enabled her to blend discipline with compassion.

Still, the move was not without hints of concern. Friends remarked she could be reserved, often turning within when life became overwhelming. She was close to her father, Fred, regularly phoning him for guidance and financial aid. Their link was solid, albeit not without strain. Fred wanted the best for her, and Maura appeared eager to live up to his expectations.

Dialogue from friends subsequently reflected her personality:

"She was fun, smart, and dependable," one friend said years later. "But sometimes, you'd see her zone out, like she was carrying something she didn't want to talk about. She wasn't the sort to disclose everything, even if you were close."

Another friend stated it differently:

"She could be the life of the party in one moment, and the next she'd be quiet, lost in thought. It wasn't moodiness—it was like her mind was somewhere else, working on something she wasn't ready to share."

This mix of tenacity, tenderness, and guardedness marked Maura Murray. She was both ordinary and extraordinary—a young lady enjoying a life full of potential but simultaneously battling with problems under the surface.

The question lingered: how much of this well-crafted persona impacted the circumstances that would lead to her disappearance?

For all her apparent success, Maura was no stranger to hardship. College life, financial strain, and personal issues weighed hard on her. Behind the façade of a disciplined student-athlete was a young lady negotiating the rough reality of early adulthood.

At UMass, Maura excelled in nursing, but her academic dedication occasionally collided with the turbulence of her life. She performed part-time campus jobs, completed tough courses, and attempted to juggle a long-distance relationship with her boyfriend, Billy. Friends recalled her managing late-night phone calls, study sessions, and social engagements with a persistent undertone of tiredness.

There were events, too, that hinted at secret conflicts. In one example, she was discovered using stolen credit card information to buy meal delivery. Though it appeared insignificant, the episode weighed hard, a blot on her otherwise immaculate record. It highlighted occasions when stress and impulse overwhelmed her generally restrained attitude.

Her friendship with Billy was another source of both comfort and distress. The two had met at West Point, and their friendship was deep, but distance taxed them. Phone conversations conveyed affection mingled with stress.

"Why didn't you tell me about that?" Billy once inquired during a late-night call, irritation in his tone.

"I didn't want to make it worse," Maura responded quietly. "You already worry too much."

Friends close to her sensed the conflict: a profound fondness for Billy, mixed with worry about the relationship's future. It was the type of anxiety many college students encounter, but in retrospect, it lent weight to the doubts about her state of mind before she went.

There were also instances of evident emotional hardship. In the days immediately leading up to her abduction, a supervisor at her campus security position recalled seeing her in tears during a shift. When asked what was wrong, she merely shook her head, unable to answer. The event was laughed aside at the moment but subsequently became a troubling detail.

Her father, Fred, was a continuous presence, occasionally arguing with her but always protective. On the weekend before her disappearance, the two met up, went vehicle shopping, and spent time together. He subsequently remembered their chats as commonplace, yet shaded by the memories of what was to come.

"She was fine," Fred remembered. "We had a good weekend. She didn't look unhappy and didn't say anything that scared me."

Still, some worried whether Maura was concealing more than she disclosed, even from her father.

By the time she packed her dorm room on February 9, 2004, and contacted instructors about a family emergency that didn't exist, the tension appeared to approach a breaking point. The delicate balance between external achievement and interior struggle looked to shatter.

Her actions—taking money from an ATM, purchasing wine, and heading north—suggested preparation, but for what? A quick escape? A strategy she hadn't revealed? Or something else entirely?

The inconsistencies were striking: a dedicated daughter, a diligent student, a loyal friend—yet also a young lady under strain, making choices that hinted at anguish under the surface.

Which version of Maura Murray genuinely characterized her final days, and how can those internal battles explain why she went without a trace?

CHAPTER 2

The Day of Disappearance

February 9, 2004, started like any other winter day in Amherst, Massachusetts, but for Maura Murray, the hours that followed would take on a disturbing importance. Snow coated the sidewalks and automobiles, the campus buzzed with the rhythm of a Monday morning, and most students concentrated on courses and routines. Yet Maura's day happened differently.

Shortly after midnight the night before, she had an unnerving phone contact with her boyfriend, Billy. The talk was not explosive, but it held the weight of unresolved tension. Billy would later remember a sensation of detachment, as if Maura's remarks were restrained.

"Is everything okay with us?" he inquired, voice tinged with anxiety.

"I just… I need some time to think," she responded, her tone quiet, almost detached.

Those remarks remained, but at the time they looked like one more kink in a long-distance relationship stressed by miles and secrets.

By daybreak, Maura seemed tranquil. She wrote an email to her instructors explaining that she would be away for the next several days owing to a reported "family emergency." The message was respectful, succinct, and compelling. Yet there was no such exigency. Her family would subsequently affirm they had no knowledge of such a claim.

She next did a succession of routine tasks—mundane behaviors that, in retrospect, seem like well-designed stages. At an ATM, she withdrew $280 in cash. At a nearby liquor shop, she bought wine and packaged booze. Surveillance video recorded her going fast, wearing a black coat, and seeming intent.

The errands may have been nothing more than preparation for a weekend away. But the accuracy of her motions aroused suspicions. Why remove practically all of her available funds? Why stock up on alcohol? And why invent a tale to her instructors if her absence was supposed to be temporary?

Later that afternoon, she packed her dorm room with a few possessions. She left behind textbooks and notes but carried toiletries, clothing, and the booze she had bought. It was a modest but crucial act: enough to hint she was contemplating a brief vacation, but not enough to indicate she was leaving her life.

A last call came in to check her voicemail, a typical action that yet implied she wanted to guarantee no loose ends.

By 4:30 p.m., Maura's Saturn car was heading north. She did not notify anybody where she was going. She did not leave a note. The buzz of the road and the oncoming darkness took her farther into New Hampshire, where the White Mountains loomed quiet and snow-covered.

The day appeared built of modest, purposeful actions—ordinary in isolation but spooky in hindsight.

The issue remained: were these the actions of a young lady seeking a brief getaway, or were they symptoms of something considerably more problematic to come?

The timing of Maura's disappearance that evening has been put together via pieces of witness testimony and government documentation. Each detail bears weight, but when combined, they produce a path of paradoxes.

At around 7:27 p.m., people along Route 112 in Haverhill, New Hampshire, heard the sound of a vehicle wreck. When they peered outside, they spotted a dark-colored Saturn car off the road, its nose jammed into a snowbank. The airbags had deployed. The automobile was Maura's.

Neighbors reported a young lady standing near the car. She seemed scared but unhurt, clothed for the winter weather. One neighbor, a school bus driver called Butch Atwood, came to provide aid.

"Do you need me to call someone?" he inquired softly, winding down his window.

"No, thank you," Maura answered, her voice calm but fast. "I've already called AAA."

Atwood thought her reaction unusual. Cell service in the region was weak, and no call to AAA was ever recorded. Still, he trusted her and proceeded home, eventually ringing the police out of worry.

Another witness, peering from a kitchen window, spotted the young lady pacing near the automobile. She appeared restless, peering up and down the road. Minutes later, when police arrived at 7:46 p.m., the Saturn stood abandoned. Maura was gone.

Inside the vehicle, cops located the alcohol she had bought; part of it was shattered, soaking the inside. Her ATM withdrawal slip and instructions to the White Mountains were also there. Missing, however, were her mobile phone, debit card, and a few personal items.

What concerned investigators most was the narrow window of time. Between 7:27 p.m. and 7:46 p.m.—barely nineteen minutes—Maura disappeared. No one saw her stroll into the woods. No passing motorist reported picking her up. No trails in the snow led to a definite destination.

Conflicting stories further exacerbated the mystery. Some neighbors stated they saw no one near the automobile after the incident. Others believed they observed a person traveling fast down the road. The timing of calls, sightings, and police presence overlapped in ways that created gaps no one could entirely reconcile.

Even the tiniest things become grounds of conflict. Did Maura appear intoxicated? Was she injured? Had she talked to anybody else before Atwood arrived? Each witness described the incident differently, leaving investigators with bits that refused to align.

One officer subsequently recalled the moment of arrival:

"It was like she just disappeared into thin air. The automobile was there, but she wasn't. No tracks led anywhere. It seemed as if the darkness swallowed her whole."

The contradictions gnawed at both police and family. If she had rushed into the woods, why leave no trail? If she had taken a ride, who was the driver—and why did no one come forward?

Every minute between the collision and the officer's arrival mattered, but those minutes stayed fuzzy, muddled by recollection, bewilderment, and stillness.

Not everything fits together clearly.

And thus the issue lingered: had Maura made a decision that night, or had someone else interfered in the last stretch of her journey?

CHAPTER 3

The Accident on Route 112

The route bent abruptly through the rural portion of Route 112 in Haverhill, New Hampshire. It was an unforgiving area to lose control of a vehicle—narrow, bordered by thick snowbanks, and poorly illuminated even in daytime. On the evening of February 9, 2004, such elements collided with a harsh winter frost and patches of black ice that lay unseen on the sidewalk.

When they heard a thump outdoors, they figured it was simply another winter accident. Collisions and skids were prevalent here. But when they walked outside to check, they noticed something unexpected.

Maura Murray's Saturn sat at an awkward angle, nose jammed into a snowbank. The front of the car displayed marks of impact—its bonnet slightly dented, the driver's side squeezed into a pile of ice and snow. Both airbags had deployed, their deflated white fabric hanging limp like mute witnesses. Headlights shone dimly against the snow, spilling wan light over the ice road.

The car's back tires stayed partly in the lane, leaving the vehicle exposed. It wasn't the horrific wreck of a high-speed accident. Instead, it seemed abrupt, as if the automobile had abruptly swerved and struck the embankment head-on.

Snow masked the noises of the night, accentuating the odd calm. No footsteps led away from the automobile. No movement moved in the nearby forests.

One neighbor, peeking from her kitchen window, noticed a figure—slender and dark-haired—standing near the truck. The individual seemed restless, going back and forth in the snow. Another neighbor claimed she observed someone leaning into the driver's side of the vehicle, as if inspecting or grabbing goods.

The situation itself was basic enough: a vehicle collision on a rural road. But the details spoke of complexity.

There was no trace of skid marks that may imply braking. No smashed glass littered the pavement, just a thin black stain from spilled liquid inside the automobile.

And as the minutes crept past, one lingering thought surfaced: was this catastrophe simply a matter of ice and chance, or had something else led Maura Murray off Route 112?

The first responder to arrive was Officer Cecil Smith of the Haverhill Police Department. The call had come in from a worried neighbor, reporting a single-vehicle collision. By the time Smith's cruiser drew up at 7:46 p.m., the Saturn was silent, headlights flickering. The individual who had been noticed near the automobile was gone.

Approaching the car, Smith instantly spotted the airbags. The deployment indicated a strong hit, albeit the front-end damage was very moderate. The driver's seat was unoccupied. Keys were missing.

Inside the automobile, some objects stuck out. An open box of Franzia wine sat in the back seat, spilling crimson liquid that damaged the upholstery. Several bottles of other alcoholic drinks were packed nearby, indicating preparation for a trip. An AAA card in Maura Murray's name was exposed, along with a few maps and written instructions for the White Mountains.

But other facts baffled Smith.

There was no evidence of blood, no smashed glass, and no indication that the driver had been gravely harmed. If Maura had been wounded, the proof wouldn't have been in the car. And if she had just walked away to get assistance, why hadn't her footsteps been apparent in the snowbanks?

Smith radioed dispatch:

"No sign of the driver. The vehicle is vacant. Requesting additional assistance."

Neighbors came carefully, providing their memories.

"She told me she already called AAA," Butch Atwood revealed. "She said she didn't need help."

Smith frowned. Cell service here was famously unstable. No record of a call exists.

Another resident shook her head. "One minute I saw her by the car; the next, she was gone. It doesn't make sense."

Smith chronicled all he could. He observed the location of the automobile, the personal possessions, and the peculiar absence of Maura herself. He investigated neighboring forests with a flashlight, shouting aloud her name. The darkness provided no reaction.

When backup came, the abnormality intensified. The automobile was locked. The driver's license and debit card were taken, but her schoolbooks remained. There was a sensation of interruption, as if someone had planned to return but never did.

Investigators then argued whether Maura had left the scene intentionally—perhaps fearing penalties of alcohol possession or a past disciplinary notice. Yet no obvious trace of her departure exists.

The unsolved questions multiplied:

Why would she tell Atwood she had already phoned for assistance? Why depart the automobile without removing anything important? And most significantly, where might she have gone in those brief minutes before police arrived?

The accident scene revealed pieces but not resolution. The gap left behind would quickly pull family, friends, and media into a frenzy of conjecture.

And thus the problem shifted: what would those closest to Maura think of her abrupt disappearance?

CHAPTER 4

Friends, Family, and the Alarm

When the evening of February 9 passed with no word from Maura Murray, no one in her family could yet understand the extent of the gathering horror. She had frequently been independent, occasionally reclusive, but seldom inaccessible.

By the next morning, her absence was no longer simply unsettling—it was worrisome. Her father, Fred Murray, was the first to recognize something was extremely wrong. He had talked with Maura just days previously, making plans for the future. Now his calls went unanswered.

"She always picked up," Fred would later recount. "If she missed a call, she called back. That's exactly how she was."

By lunchtime, the family decided they had to act. Friends on campus were contacted. Professors were asked whether they had heard anything. The responses were exactly the same: no one had seen or talked with Maura since the day before.

The revelation struck in with a weight that none of them could shake. Something had occurred.

Fred phoned officials in New Hampshire, where Maura's vehicle had been located. It was the beginning of the official process. The words "missing person" carried a chilling gravity. For the family, they marked the shift from worry to dread.

Kathleen Murray, Maura's sister, described the moment she learned her sister was missing.

"I thought it was a mistake. I assumed maybe she had simply gone to clear her brain. But then… the hours kept passing."

The family mobilized swiftly. Phone calls were made, questions were asked, and messages were left on voicemail after voicemail. Friends were dragged into the endeavor, seeking any hint of where Maura may have gone or why.

Her lover, Billy, stationed at Fort Sill in Oklahoma, heard the sad news. His voice broke when he chatted on the phone with Fred.

"I'll come as soon as I can," Billy assured. "Just tell me where to go."

Each hour seemed like a race against time. The frigid weather, the desolate roads, and the rural isolation—all exacerbated the urgency. Missing people cases are usually solved in the first twenty-four hours. By then, Maura had already been gone for almost a whole night.

As Fred traveled north to New Hampshire, the scenery blurred with his thoughts. Was she hurt? Was she hiding? Has someone stolen her?

The first missing person report was submitted, solidifying the transformation from panic to formal catastrophe.

Yet even as the paperwork was finalized, one persistent concern dogged those closest to her: what may have occurred in those important early hours when Maura might have still been found?

As detectives started collecting statements from family, friends, and bystanders, flaws surfaced in the narratives. Small pieces of information opposed one another. Timelines altered depending on who told them.

Fred Murray recalled his last weekend with Maura differently at times, describing plans, discussions, and her mood in ways that didn't always align with other family recollections. Some regarded her as optimistic, looking forward to the semester. Others felt she was silent, unfocused, and carrying burdens she wasn't ready to reveal.

Friends provided similarly inconsistent images. One roommate recalls Maura stating she "just needed a break." Another maintained she hadn't mentioned any vacation at all.

The differences weren't always indicators of deceit—memory under stress sometimes falters. Yet they generated a shroud that hindered the research.

Witness testimonies from Route 112 provided another depth. Some neighbors swear they spotted Maura near the automobile. Others weren't convinced it was her. One characterized her as serene, while another felt she seemed disturbed.

Even inside the family, emotions occasionally distorted perspective. Kathleen reported one version of events concerning their final discussion; Julie, another sister, recalled it differently. Reporters who subsequently went through interviews remarked how these discrepancies reinforced the mystery. If even those closest to Maura could not agree on her state of mind or intentions, how could investigators predict her next steps?

At a news conference days later, dissatisfaction appeared.

A journalist questioned Fred directly, "Do you think Maura ran away?"

Fred's answer was harsh. "My daughter didn't run away. Something happened to her, and somebody knows what it was."

Behind the hardness, however, investigators felt doubt. Each contradicting detail—each variance in testimony—was another thread they had to disentangle.

The longer they listened, the more perplexing the image got. Had Maura planned a brief leave from school, or something more permanent? Did her family know her better than anyone—or did they not even completely realize what was hurting her?

The discrepancies did not merely complicate the search. They hinted at greater riddles, ones that could not be resolved by recollection alone. And thus, with the initial layers of testimony collected, the attention switched toward law enforcement's part. What would the official probe show that personal memories could not?

CHAPTER 5

The Investigation Begins

When Officer Cecil Smith arrived on Route 112 and discovered Maura Murray's vehicle abandoned, the clock began ticking on one of New Hampshire's most confusing missing person cases. The coming hours and days would influence the direction of the search, and retrospect would disclose both dedicated efforts and disturbing gaps.

At first, the event was treated like a regular single-vehicle collision. Smith investigated the site, got comments from adjacent people, and observed the empty automobile. His original report registered the collision at 7:46 p.m., less than 20 minutes after the impact was initially heard. But the driver—Maura—was nowhere in sight.

Within hours, Haverhill Police called local dispatch to investigate surrounding hospitals. No patient matching Maura's description had been admitted. Officers combed the local area with spotlights, shouting out her name into the chilly darkness. There was no reaction.

The next morning, the hunt increased. Law enforcement conducted a ground search with police, K-9 units, and volunteers. An aircraft outfitted with infrared equipment surveyed the snow-covered woods, seeking for body heat that would suggest someone hiding or slumped in the cold.

"We'll expand the grid," one cop remarked as they sketched out quadrants of property surrounding Route 112.

But as the hours passed, rescuers discovered no tracks going away from the vehicle and no evidence of Maura in the deep forest. Snow had partly filled in overnight, concealing any traces.

The lack of a clear trace seemed perplexing. In most rural disappearances, search dogs at least capture a scent. Here, the dogs lost it within a short distance of the automobile, as if Maura had suddenly disappeared off the wayside.

Timelines were reviewed. Calls to AAA revealed no request for roadside assistance had been made. Neighbors' reports differed, with some saying they saw her near the truck and others doubtful.

By midweek, New Hampshire Fish and Game joined the endeavor, adding extra people and search equipment. Maps of the White Mountains were researched. Did she plan to hike? Was she hiding away in a cabin? Search leaders evaluated every option.

And yet, the huge net delivered nothing substantial. No clothes were recovered, no discarded objects, and no trail to pursue.

The early answer was comprehensive in appearance but limiting in scope. Much of the effort centered on the local region surrounding the accident site. If Maura had departed by vehicle with someone else, the search radius would have been meaningless.

As one disgruntled family member subsequently put it:

"They searched the woods like she had wandered off. But what if she never ventured into the woods at all?"

The key issue loomed: with so many resources devoted so swiftly, how could the search yield no sign of Maura Murray?

Parallel to the hunt, police shifted their focus to the Saturn itself—the final tangible connection to Maura. The car was removed to a safe place for investigation.

Inside, they photographed the box of Franzia wine, the scattered bottles, and a crimson stain consistent with spilled alcohol. Maps and printed instructions to the White Mountains lie on the passenger seat. But the goods most crucial to understanding her movements—her mobile phone, debit card, and keys—were gone.

Forensics teams sought to dust for fingerprints and other trace evidence. Yet the findings were inconclusive. Maura's prints were anticipated; others were not readily recognized. Snow and wetness have degraded surfaces.

The airbags were checked. Their deployment verified a moderate collision, but not one likely to inflict major harm. The lack of blood bolstered the assumption that Maura walked away uninjured.

Investigators also noticed that the driver's side window seemed damaged and that a rag had been shoved into the tailpipe—a detail that prompted dispute. Some assumed it was an effort to attract less notice from authorities by disguising exhaust smoke. Others said it may have been a hint of an automobile issue early in the journey.

Technical obstacles exacerbated the inquiry. Cell phone records from 2004 were not as detailed as contemporary data, making it difficult to locate Maura's actual position during her final known conversations. Bank records validated her ATM withdrawal and purchases, but they supplied no indications regarding her location.

One officer characterized the frustration:

"We had the car, but the car wasn't talking. It provided us with bits, not answers."

Family members feel key chances were lost. The automobile was returned back to the family quite soon, restricting additional forensic analysis. Neighbors' yards were not adequately examined in the initial vital days. Surveillance cameras from surrounding businesses were either unavailable or not gathered.

Even the K-9 units, one of the most promising instruments, achieved modest results. Dogs apparently traced a scent approximately 100 yards east of the automobile before losing it suddenly, near the junction of Bradley Hill Road. That quick halt sparked speculations that Maura may have entered another car.

Yet the absence of concrete proof left detectives groping. No footsteps, no smell trail beyond the small span, no objects abandoned in panic—all of it contributed to the eerie vacuum.

The forensic quiet was deafening. In an era before modern DNA analysis, before extensive digital monitoring, detectives were left with a vehicle that told half a tale and a trail that stopped too quickly.

And so, with the technical leads running cold, focus moved elsewhere. If science could not supply answers, perhaps hypotheses and guesswork might.

But what tale would those hypotheses tell about Maura Murray's fate?

CHAPTER 6

Theories Emerge

From the very first hours of Maura Murray's disappearance, questions outweighed answers. Each quiet in the data, each gap in the timetable, provided fertile ground for supposition. Over time, three basic ideas gained prominence: that she succumbed to the elements after an accident, that she went away to start over, or that she fell victim to foul play.

Each explanation seemed credible in its own way, and yet none supplied a convincing narrative.

Theory One: The Accident and Exposure

The earliest and possibly most basic interpretation was that Maura had fled the accident site willingly but fatally misunderstood the perils of the cold night. In this scenario, after wrecking the Saturn on Route 112, she went off on foot to evade detection—perhaps frightened of legal ramifications, given the alcohol in her vehicle and the likelihood of probation troubles from earlier minor charges.

The temperature that evening had fallen considerably below freezing. Snow coated the wayside, and the woods were still safe for the creak of ice. A person trekking without suitable clothes may rapidly get lost and succumb to hypothermia.

"Maybe she just panicked," one search volunteer surmised years later. "You're young, you've been drinking, and you don't want to get in trouble. So you run. But out there, you don't get far."

This notion acquired legitimacy given the history of comparable occurrences in the White Mountains, when trekkers overestimated the elements. Searchers, however, were mystified by the absence of proof. No footsteps led away from the automobile. Dogs followed her smell only momentarily before it disappeared. A complete ground and aircraft scan produced nothing.

If she had slumped close, why didn't infrared scans identify her? If she had made it further, why wasn't her corpse recovered in future searches? The forests near Haverhill were thick, but not limitless. A tangible trace, even years later, would be anticipated.

The accident scenario explained her initial absence but failed to account for the lingering stillness following.

Theory Two: The Runaway

Another strain of thought claimed Maura's disappearance was purposeful. The days before she disappeared carried evidence of mental anguish. She had put her dorm room items into boxes, texted instructors with a spurious claim of a family emergency, and shopped online for rental apartments in New Hampshire.

To some, this appeared like preparation. Perhaps she hoped to start afresh, away from academic stress and emotional hardship. The White Mountains may provide escape—anonymity in little communities, seasonal occupations, and limitless routes where someone could stay unknown.

Her ATM withdrawal of $280, together with her booze purchase, showed she was sponsoring a brief escape.

"Sometimes people just want out," one investigator mused. "College, relationships, family expectations—it all piles up. She was knowledgeable enough to plot an exit."

But the runaway idea brought its own problems. Why leave her vehicle, her debit card, and her phone? If she had arranged for someone to take her up, where was the proof? And if her purpose was escape, why use a tactic likely to ignite a police search and worldwide attention?

Moreover, no documented sightings of Maura ever emerged. Not in little towns, not in hiking hostels, nor over the border into Canada. A successful escape needed resources and stealth. Did a 21-year-old student have either?

The runaway idea was intriguing because it explained motivation. Yet it necessitated a level of execution that appeared contradictory to the chaos of the disaster.

Theory Three: Foul Play

The most horrifying notion indicated that Maura had not departed of her own will but had been stolen. This theory gained momentum from the uncanny features of the case: the dogs losing her scent suddenly at a crossroads crossing, the utter lack of physical evidence, and the absence of tracks in new snow.

If she had taken a ride from a passing motorist—or worse, been forced into a vehicle—it may explain the rapid shutdown.

The rural part of Route 112 was secluded. Cars were scarce, but not absent. A stranger or even an acquaintance may have stopped, provided aid, or taken advantage of her weakness.

"Somebody picked her up," one family member stated plainly. "That's the only thing that makes sense."

This idea sparked more troubling questions: Who would have been on that route at that moment? Did someone local know the region well enough to disappear without notice? Was it an opportunistic act or something planned?

The difficulty was evidence. There were no witnesses to an abduction, no physical struggle at the spot, and no forensic clues within the Saturn pointing to criminal activity. Investigators have hypotheses, but theories are not proof.

And yet, of all possibilities, foul play accounted best for the lingering mystery: a disappearance with no trace, no corpse, and no explanations.

Each hypothesis held weight. Each hypothesis contained weaknesses. The question persisted for the public, the family, and investigators alike:

Which of these pathways provides the actual tale of what occurred to Maura Murray on Route 112?

As the weeks turned into months, the silence of facts created a vacuum that conjecture hurried to fill. The Maura Murray case started to garner national media attention, and with it came a maelstrom of hypotheses, disputes, and allegations.

Television programs showed her happy college photographs against the dismal roadway where her vehicle was recovered. Online forums exploded with armchair detectives dissecting every aspect of her final days. Each crumb of information—real or rumored—was analyzed, argued, and stored.

For Maura's family, the attention was both a lifeline and a pain.

"We needed people to know her face," her father, Fred, stated. "We needed the case alive. But at the same time, it seemed like the world was evaluating her without knowing her."

Media narratives affected public view. One headline presented her as a distressed student escaping personal troubles. Another depicted her as a victim of a mystery predator. Each approach held ramifications for how investigators prioritized leads.

Police faced increased pressure. Tips rushed in, most of them unreliable. Strangers reported sightings from

46

Vermont to Canada. Psychics sent letters recounting visions. Every unconfirmed allegation devoured time and resources, diverting from solid proof.

The conjecture also fostered divisiveness within the society. Some residents opposed the incursion, arguing that outsiders overstated threats in their little village. Others feared a predator among them. The uncertainty undermined trust.

Conversations typically held an air of discomfort.

"You think she just walked off?" one person asked another at the local supermarket.

"Not a chance," was the reply. "Somebody out there knows something. Maybe somebody is right here."

The internet magnified every rumor. Anonymous commenters accused family members of concealing truths. Others claimed firsthand knowledge of the night she disappeared. None of it could be verified, but once online, conjecture became permanent, altering the case in ways that investigators could not ignore.

Over time, the coverage acquired its own momentum. Maura's disappearance became less a single case and more a national mystery—a conundrum the public felt entitled to solve.

And yet, for all the commotion, the key issues remained unaddressed. The truth was buried under layers of theory, supposition, and narrative manipulation.

As the inquiry reached its next phase, focus moved on individuals—those who had been at the scene, those who knew Maura, and those whose tales did not exactly line up.

If the hypotheses alone did not settle the issue, then identifying prospective suspects may.

But would that quest yield answers—or merely deepen the shadows?

CHAPTER 7

Suspects and Leads

The inquiry into Maura Murray's disappearance ultimately moved toward people—those who knew her, those who lived along Route 112, and anybody whose behavior on February 9, 2004, raised doubts. Law enforcement, urged by the public for progress, inspected many people of interest. Some were inspected carefully, interrogated, and cleared. Others remained in the shadows of suspicion, their names murmured in forums and documentaries long after official files moved on.

The Local Witnesses

The first obvious focus was the individuals who saw Maura that night. Butch Atwood, the school bus driver who came across the Saturn, told investigators he stopped, pulled down his window, and offered to call for assistance.

"She looked shaken, but she told me not to call anyone," Atwood later remembered. "She said she'd already called AAA. I knew that wasn't possible, not out here. But she insisted."

Atwood drove on and parked at his house less than a hundred yards away. From his window, he claimed to have kept an eye out for cops. Within minutes, the responding officer arrived. Maura, however, was gone.

For years, doubters online examined Atwood's testimony. Why didn't he insist on assisting her? Why did she refuse? Could he have played a role? Police interrogated him many times, including examining his property, but found no proof of criminality. In the official perspective, he was only a concerned onlooker.

Yet suspicions persisted in the popular imagination: Had Atwood seen more than he admitted? Or was he just the last unfortunate person to observe Maura alive?

Family Scrutiny

Inevitably, mistrust shifted inward. Families in missing person instances are generally probed first. Maura's father, Fred Murray, faced challenging questions in interviews. His vigorous pursuit for answers—confronting police officials, contacting journalists, demanding searches—struck some as resolve, others as defensiveness.

"I'm not hiding anything," Fred stated in one TV interview. "All I want is my daughter back."

Investigators uncovered nothing tying him or other family members to Maura's disappearance. Still, murmurs spread online, encouraged by the tiniest irregularities.

In actuality, what seemed strange to outsiders was frequently simply the raw sadness of a parent living in constant limbo.

The Boyfriend and West Point Ties

Attention also focused on Maura's lover, Bill Rausch, an Army lieutenant at Fort Sill, Oklahoma. Their relationship, long-distance and allegedly tense, was analyzed by both police and amateur sleuths. Phone records indicated that Bill had attempted repeatedly to contact Maura after she went missing, leaving frantic voicemails.

"She's the love of my life," he told a journalist. "If anyone thinks I'd hurt her, they don't know me."

Still, the military background and the strain of a difficult relationship create shadows. Some alluded to emails exchanged between them, hinting at conflict. Others emphasized subsequent charges about Bill's conduct, years after Maura's disappearance, as potential character proof.

But technically, he was never prosecuted, and law enforcement discovered no clear connection between him and the events of that night.

Neighbors and Locals

Several local citizens also came under examination. One neighbor claimed to have observed a person walking fast near the collision scene, albeit their description was imprecise. Another reported hearing a noise that sounded like a vehicle door slamming.

Police followed up, canvassing the tiny community. Rumors circulate about persons with criminal records in the neighborhood. One individual with past charges was questioned extensively but cleared following alibi verification.

Yet, as one cop said privately, "We can't rule out the possibility that someone local saw an opportunity. But proving it? That's another matter."

The Mysterious Phone Call

Complicating things was an odd lead involving a guy who apparently phoned a local police agency years later, claiming to have knowledge regarding Maura's fate. The caller's specifics were vague, his objectives ambiguous, and nothing definite surfaced.

The absence of follow-up proof rendered the tip a dead end. But the sheer presence of such calls kept suspicion alive—if someone knew anything, why hide behind anonymous whispers?

By the conclusion of the first year, detectives had met with dozens of persons, ruled out others, and kept a few under covert surveillance. Yet the key question remained unanswered:

Did one of these folks have the missing piece to Maura Murray's story?

For every lead that sounded promising, the investigators met twice as many dead ends. Each false start chipped away at morale, leaving investigators—and Maura's family—frustrated by the silence of the facts.

The Abandoned House

Early in the hunt, dogs followed Maura's scent to a neighboring residence. The lead excited investigators. Could she have sought sanctuary there? Could foul play have happened inside?

Officers investigated the premises extensively, finding nothing. No sign of Maura. No indications of a struggle. The impact, they subsequently speculated, may have been contamination by handlers or other odors. Still, the tale of "the suspicious house" circulated fast across forums, feeding suspicion for years.

The Canadian Border Theory

Some speculated that Maura had slipped into Canada, sneaking away unobserved. The notion bore superficial appeal—the border was a few hours' drive, and she had shown interest in the White Mountains earlier.

But her passport stayed behind. No reliable sightings appeared over the border. Border patrol data produced nothing. Without evidence, the Canadian escape scenario crumbled into another diversion.

The Alleged Sightings

In the weeks following her disappearance, multiple individuals claimed to have seen Maura in adjacent towns. A young lady resembling her was reported at a convenience shop. Another report indicated someone matching her description at a pub in Vermont.

Investigators pursued each lead, analyzing security video when feasible and questioning witnesses. Each time, the outcome was the same: not Maura.

"Every sighting was like a spark of hope," one officer acknowledged. "And every time, it burned out."

Internet Sleuths and False Trails

As the case gathered attention online, amateur investigators submitted theories—sometimes smart, sometimes destructive. Unverified rumors accused residents of complicity. Others theorized about concealed pregnancies, secret lifestyles, or conspiracies, including police cover-ups.

Each rumor pushed investigators to commit resources, investigating assertions that went nowhere. For the family, reading unfounded charges online increased their grief.

"They don't know what it's like," Fred Murray remarked. "They sit at a computer, spinning stories, while we're living this nightmare."

The Recovered Bones

Years later, bones uncovered in the area generated fresh hope of closure. Testing proved they were not Maura's. Another false lead, another emotional breakdown for the family.
The pattern of research grew disturbingly repetitive: a lead, a burst of optimism, an extensive pursuit, and then—nothing. Each red herring not only delayed the truth but also strengthened the case's air of impenetrability.

As one investigator put it frankly, "Every time we thought we were close, the trail evaporated."

The unsolved question remained:

If none of these suspicions or leads yielded answers, was the solution to Maura's disappearance resting elsewhere—perhaps in the hands of the same public currently worrying over her fate?

CHAPTER 8

Online Sleuths and Public Obsession

Long before social media platforms like Facebook and TikTok were everyday fixtures, the disappearance of Maura Murray unfolded on message boards and discussion forums. It was 2004, the early years of the internet's spread into genuine crime. By the time mainstream media moved on from the case, internet groups had already started portraying Maura's disappearance as a puzzle to be solved, a riddle that any dedicated outsider might help crack.

Websleuths became one of the key sites where Maura's case was deconstructed line by line. Members from across the globe joined threads devoted solely to her tale. They pored over maps of Route 112, fought over whether her automobile accident was manufactured or real, and theorized endlessly about what type of person Maura genuinely was. One commenter remarked late at night, "Look at the timing. The bus driver exits, and she disappears in minutes. That can't be a coincidence." Others countered by defending witnesses, suggesting that suspicion cast too wide only diluted the investigation.

Crowdsourced suggestions poured into police stations, sometimes overloading detectives. People wrote letters and sent emails stating they had found out where Maura had gone. A guy in Vermont said he had seen her at a tavern. A lady in Maine was certain she had seen her in a grocery store aisle. Each account was followed up, although all ended in disappointment. The trend was clear: internet groups could produce huge energy, but most of it evaporated into false leads.

Still, there were occasions when the collective effort did something helpful. Forum members built precise timelines, matching phone records, ATM video, and witness testimony into logical images. Some made maps overlaying various walking paths Maura may have taken following her accident. Others spotted contradictions in official news statements, which subsequently prompted the media to pursue harder questions of police.

Yet the usefulness of these online contributions came at a cost. Names of innocent residents spread widely, tied to suspicions they could never escape. One family living near the accident scene was accused by anonymous commenters of harboring Maura in their basement. The story got such momentum that their property was hounded with phone calls and internet harassment. When investigators exonerated the family, the harm had already been done.

On one site, a dispute lasted late into the night.

"She staged the crash. I'm telling you, she wanted to disappear," wrote one anonymous user.

Another shot back: "No. Someone snatched her. Look at the time. She couldn't have merely vanished."

And from a third came the warning: "Speculation isn't evidence. If we blame everyone, no one will trust the truth when it comes up."

The talk demonstrated the twin character of internet obsession: a thirst for answers mixed with a contempt for bounds.

As years passed, internet attention went beyond forums. Blogs arose, recording every piece of evidence available. Some bloggers positioned themselves as independent investigators, obtaining police papers under Freedom of Information legislation and reporting their results. Podcasts eventually added another dimension, dedicating full seasons to the case. Each medium amplified public attention but also provided fresh interpretations and distortions.

By 2010, Maura's situation was no longer isolated to New Hampshire or Massachusetts. It had become worldwide, a digital riddle that strangers thousands of miles away argued as if they were eyewitnesses. The united energy was obvious. The issue was whether it was genuinely helping—or clouding the reality.

Could a case so intensely analyzed by strangers possibly be solved when every new idea appeared to drown the evidence in louder speculation?

The development of "armchair detectives" was both a phenomenon and a concern. These amateur detectives, equipped with computers and tenacity, felt they could locate what police had overlooked. Some had legitimate skills—backgrounds in cartography, data analysis, or psychology—that offered insight to the conversation. Others brought just gut feeling and distrust.

The contrast between supposition and reality became a distinguishing characteristic of the case's digital afterlife. For every properly researched post, there were five others inspired by gossip. Innocent slip-ups in witness testimonies were magnified into charges. Family members of Maura, already living in uncertainty, frequently felt targeted by the very groups professing to desire answers.

Fred Murray himself showed both thankfulness and displeasure. "I appreciate that people care," he stated in one interview, his voice husky. "But it's hard, seeing strangers tear apart every detail of her life, like they know her better than we did."

Inside the forums, disagreements regularly degenerated into vitriol. Arguments erupted over the slightest details: the time of a phone conversation, the exact angle of the wrecked Saturn, and the interpretation of an eyewitness statement. Moderators battled to keep debates respectful. Many threads ended up locked and archived, not because they had solved anything, but because they had devoured themselves in circular discussions.

The boundary between useful input and damaging conjecture blurred further with the introduction of real crime films. When "Disappeared" presented Maura's case in 2009, attention increased considerably. New users invaded forums, rehashing notions previously contested years before. The cycle repeated: accusations, rebuttals, wounded emotions, and more noise added to an already congested environment.

One person responded in exasperation: "We're just chasing ghosts. Every time I think we're onto something, someone else pulls it apart. Maybe that's why the cops don't listen to us."

Another said bluntly, "If we don't push, no one will. Cases like these become cold because everyone's too terrified to keep asking questions."

The contradiction was evident. The internet groups kept the case alive in the public spotlight, ensuring Maura Murray's name was not forgotten. Without them, her tale could have disappeared into the lengthy list of unexplained disappearances. But at the same time, the conjecture frequently disguised what little evidence existed, burying facts behind speculations.

Investigators recognized the mixed effect. While recommendations sometimes revealed fresh avenues, most were dead ends. Police resources, already tight, were strained further by the necessity to assess every item of public feedback. Some police stated privately that they avoided communicating with internet sleuths completely.

The fixation reached a point where people showed up in Haverhill, traversing Route 112 with cameras, recreating Maura's final steps. Some knocked on the doors of residents, demanding explanations. A handful even dug near homes, certain they could find the facts themselves.

Residents became uncomfortable. "They're turning our town into a crime scene," one neighbor told a reporter.

"Every stranger that comes here thinks they're going to solve it. But all they're doing is stirring things up."

And still, the digital chase persisted, spurred by the mystery's sheer reluctance to be solved.

The persistent tension posed a frightening question: were these internet efforts keeping the search alive, or were they burying the truth behind layers of ceaseless noise?

CHAPTER 9

Long-Term Investigations

The years went on, and with them came the weight of quiet. Maura Murray's disappearance, once a headline-grabbing mystery, drifted into the unsettling world of cold cases. Officially, the investigation never closed. Her file remained current, her name still held weight in law enforcement briefings, but the cadence of fresh leads dropped until they practically ceased completely.

Police returned occasionally to Route 112, strolling the same tiny section of road where her Saturn had been left behind. They interviewed people more than once, anticipating that recollections may evolve or strengthen with time. Sometimes they repeated the same questions, just rephrased, examining if a feature earlier ignored may emerge. "We're not here to accuse you," one cop informed a lifelong resident, recorder in hand. "We're here because memories change. Maybe you'll recall something now that you didn't before."

But answers seldom arrived.

Every few years, police enforcement declares a fresh endeavor. Search dogs combed the forested landscape again and again. Cadaver dogs were brought in, their masters walking them over melting earth in spring and frozen ground in winter. Aerial assessments were undertaken, employing drones to examine the forest's density. Each endeavor increased public optimism, only to end in quiet despair when nothing appeared.

The cold case designation did not signify abandonment—it signified tenacity without progress. In the lack of clear proof, investigators explored notions previously deconstructed by both experts and amateurs. Did Maura escape voluntarily? Was she stolen by someone in the brief minutes between the bus driver's departure and police arrival? Could she have disappeared into the woods, succumbing to the elements?

Detectives went over the same inquiries, circling them like orbiting planets that never collided.

At one point, officials dug up a property in the Haverhill region after indications indicated Maura's corpse could have been hidden there. Cameras captured the hunt; journalists gathered on the perimeter. When nothing was uncovered, authorities reassured the public that they would continue pursuing reliable information. But the inability to uncover anything just exacerbated the feeling of hopelessness.

One veteran cop, thinking years later, said softly to a colleague, "We've looked under every stone. If the solution was there, we should've discovered it by now."

The colleague answered, almost whispering, "Or maybe we just haven't looked under the right one."

Technology, too, has become part of the investigative cycle. Early 2000s approaches had limitations that irritated cops at the time. DNA recovery was less sensitive; digital data were less accessible. As years passed, officials started scrutinizing artifacts seized from the Saturn, pondering whether they should be examined again. Every piece of evidence—seatbelt fibers, probable fingerprints, trace materials—was studied under the prism of contemporary science.

Yet even such steps presented obstacles. Some objects decayed over time; others lacked adequate material for testing. Investigators confronted the painful dilemma of current cold case work: the technologies were now refined enough to locate answers, yet the evidence could have drifted too far into decay to be meaningful.

Families of the missing seldom obtain updates with satisfactory closure. Instead, they suffer extended intervals between short phone conversations or letters. Fred Murray defined these pauses as "waiting rooms of grief"—periods of quiet interrupted only by fresh optimism when a search or forensic review was announced.

Still, perseverance mattered. Authorities did not shut the file. They investigated leads, ran names through databases, and tested unidentifiable remains against Maura's dental records and DNA. Each step recognized that although time veiled the truth, the potential of discovery still persisted.

But as the second decade without answers drew in, the same nagging question became louder: if conventional tactics had given nothing, might new investigative tools ultimately break through the silence?

By the 2010s, forensic technology had improved at a speed that outstripped the early days of Maura's case. What formerly needed massive quantities of DNA might now be accomplished with a tiny quantity. Touch DNA—skin cells left behind by the briefest contact—became a game-changing technology.

Investigators wondered: might anything on the Saturn, long neglected, finally disclose a profile?

Digital databases grew as well. CODIS, the national DNA index, expanded with every conviction and upload. NamUs, a database for missing individuals and unidentified remains, offers novel cross-referencing possibilities. Law enforcement may now compare Maura's information against instances around the nation with remarkable speed.

Even genealogy evolved as a forensic weapon. The Golden State Killer case, solved in 2018 with DNA relatives located on consumer ancestry sites, altered the landscape altogether. Families long thought remote might now build a link going back to an unknown culprit. Some worried that if Maura had been abused and the culprit left DNA, genealogy may one day reveal them.

A detective asked about cold cases and remarked plainly, "We're playing a long game now. Science is catching up to puzzles that defeated us twenty years ago."

Not all investigators were similarly positive. DNA required a sample, and Maura's case lacked a visible crime scene. The automobile yielded scant information, and there was no proven evidence of foul activity at the place of her abduction. The forests provided nothing.

Without a person, without a weapon, science has nothing to connect itself to.

And yet, improvements kept optimism alive. Digital techniques enabled investigators to re-analyze Maura's mobile phone data. Mapping algorithms might recreate her probable travel path with more accuracy. Artificial intelligence techniques were used to find trends in missing people data, comparing Maura's case to others countrywide.

Online, aficionados jumped onto every rumor of new forensic procedures. Forums hummed with posts: "What if they test the seatbelts again with touch DNA?" Others reacted with doubt: "If they had anything, they would've told us by now."

In one private exchange between two investigators, the exasperation was evident.

"We're always one step behind," stated the first. "Every time the tech improves, we realize we should've kept more, preserved more. But twenty years ago, we didn't know what we'd need."

The second sighed. "Science can't fix what wasn't collected. But it may still surprise us. Sometimes all it takes is one missed trace."

The confidence that science may yet break the case was not restricted to specialists. Families of the missing increasingly campaigned for forensic evaluations, requesting retests of decades-old material. For Fred Murray, the issue was not whether technology might assist, but whether authorities would use it with haste.

"We don't need promises," he told a reporter. "We need results. If the science is there, utilize it. Don't wait until I'm gone to discover my daughter."

And thus the case lies at a crossroads—between the weight of two decades of failure and the light of contemporary science's reach.

Will DNA, databases, or digital forensics ultimately discover the truth about what occurred on Route 112? Or will Maura Murray's disappearance remain one of the few mysteries that even science cannot close?

CHAPTER 10

Theories, Controversies, and Legacy

The years have done nothing to smooth the rough edges of Maura Murray's disappearance. If anything, time has just intensified the mystery. For every truth proven, another question stays unsolved. For every hypothesis offered, conflicts and blind spots persist. What occurred on that frigid February evening on Route 112 has become a mystery without a solution, a riddle that refuses to give its reality.

The known facts are plain enough: Maura left her dorm room at the University of Massachusetts Amherst on February 9, 2004. She drove her Saturn north, bringing personal goods, cash, and drink. She smashed the automobile near Haverhill, New Hampshire, and within a brief window of time—no more than a few minutes—she disappeared. Witnesses spotted her at the site, and then she was gone.

But what lies beyond those facts is obscure, fractured, and passionately contested.

Some claim she walked into the woods, overwhelmed and likely inebriated, and succumbed to the elements. Yet no sign of her has ever been located, despite exhaustive searches. Others assume she was picked up by someone traveling down Route 112—a stranger, or possibly an acquaintance. But if such were the case, why has no proof arisen in almost two decades?

Theories of voluntary disappearance , too. Did Maura plan to start a new life someplace far away? Her packed possessions show planning, although she left behind her credit cards, and phone activity unexpectedly ended. Could she have arranged her own disappearance, or was she deprived of the opportunity by a perilous meeting she never anticipated?

Even the simplest things generate suspicion.

Why did she choose Route 112, a remote route with no clear goal for her? Why did she not withdraw money from her ATM earlier that day if she was planning a trip? Why, when the bus driver offered aid, did she decline?

Investigators have gone in circles with these queries, knowing that the answers may never surface.

In a private interview years after the incident, one investigator acknowledged to a colleague:

"We know where she started. We know where she stopped. But everything in between is shadows."

The colleague remarked gravely, "And the shadows may be all we ever get."

What makes Maura's case truly troubling is how it refuses to settle into one coherent narrative. Every theory creates holes, and every option opens paradoxes. To this day, conversations online and in law enforcement agencies repeat the same refrain: what, precisely, are we missing?

And maybe the most uncomfortable issue of all is if the truth is something that will never be settled.

Maura Murray's disappearance did not simply affect her family; it transformed a town and resonated throughout the ethos of real crime investigation itself.

For her father, Fred Murray, the lawsuit became the defining fight of his life. He confronted law enforcement constantly, asked for documents, and blasted what he felt were wasted chances in the early probe. His perseverance kept the matter alive in the public spotlight, even when years passed without formal progress.

Friends characterized Fred's effort as both inspirational and tragic. "He's never stopped," one remarked in an interview. "Even when everyone else was , even when the news cameras left, he was still out there."

For Maura's siblings, the grief was worsened by public scrutiny. They lived through conjecture not just about what happened to their sister, but about her character, her choices, and her secrets. The internet reinforced every rumor, forcing them to mourn under a spotlight.

The community of Haverhill, too, was transformed. A sleepy community suddenly found itself the center of national media interest. Residents were interrogated, their homes examined, and their habits interrupted. Many were leery of strangers, especially when internet sleuths started visiting the crash site in quest of clues.

And yet, beyond the emotional toll, the case altered the culture of real crime itself.

In the early 2000s, when podcasts and streaming documentaries ruled the landscape, Maura's disappearance became one of the first mysteries to burst online. Forums packed with conjecture. Amateur investigators published timetables, maps, and speculations, often rivaling official records in detail. The internet fixation blurred the barrier between popular interest and investigative effort.

Some applauded it as a new type of community-driven justice; others decried it as irresponsible conjecture that frequently injured the family more than it helped.

Still, Maura's story revealed the persistent obsession with unexplained disappearances. It illustrated how a single mystery, with just enough clues to tantalize but not enough to solve, could engage viewers for decades. In that sense, her impact reaches well beyond her personal story—it symbolizes the greater human yearning for answers, for closure, for the missing piece that explains the unexplainable.

In a moment of introspection during an interview, a reporter once asked Fred Murray, "What do you think Maura's case has taught people?"

Fred hesitated, his voice low. "That you can lose someone in a heartbeat, and the world won't stop to help you find them. You have to battle for every shred of truth. And even then, you may never grasp it."

The message resonates beyond one family, beyond one situation. It touches on the fragility of justice, the limitations of research, and the durability of human mystery.

Nearly two decades later, the curiosity persists. Documentaries revisit the chronology. Podcasts analyze the theories. Online conversations continue, pulling in new generations of listeners and readers. Each recounting offers the same hope: that one forgotten detail would finally shatter the quiet.

But the question continues, repeating like a mantra at the conclusion of every hypothesis, every argument, every contemplation on legacy—

Will we ever fully know what happened to Maura Murray?

EPILOGUE

Vanished but Not Forgotten

The disappearance of Maura Murray is one of the most intriguing of contemporary real crime. Despite intensive investigations, innumerable interviews, and over two decades of conjecture, the trail has never provided the answer her family—and the world—had waited for.

Maura's story is not merely the narrative of a young lady who disappeared on a chilly February night. It is also the tale of a family's tenacious battle for answers, a town caught in the spotlight of national attention, and a case that altered how the public deals with unsolved murders. Every year that passes, the solitude along Route 112 gets heavier, and the questions echo louder: Why did she travel north? Who, if anybody, encountered her along that road? And how could a young lady go so totally without a trace?

Her legacy resides not just in the questions left behind but in the tremendous influence her case has had on the culture of research, media, and internet communities. Maura's disappearance has come to represent both the fragility of truth and the perseverance of those who refuse to let it be forgotten.

The cost has been immense—measured in restless nights, countless hypotheses, shattered relationships, and the constant anguish of absence. It is a reminder that behind every headline and every mystery lies a real existence, once lively and full of hope.

And yet, the persistent impact of Maura's tale guarantees she is not lost to time. She lives in remembrance, in vigilance, and in the continual hope that one day, the stillness will shatter.

Speculation has always surrounded this case, and although hypotheses abound, few are anchored on reality. Some suspect Maura engineered the disappearance, referring to her reclusive conduct before leaving college. Yet proof for such a plot is thin—she left her bank accounts undisturbed, her phone deactivated, and her relatives dubious she planned to go permanently.

Others feel foul play is the only logical scenario, envisioning a stranger or possibly a local resident saw her after the incident. While unsettling, no forensic evidence has confirmed this accusation, and no suspect has ever been prosecuted.

The most devastating possibility—that Maura died to the elements after fleeing the accident site—remains impossible to reject. But numerous searches, with dogs, aircraft, and ground teams, failed to find even the tiniest trace.

This is the line between fact and supposition. Verified documents offer us a precise timeline: the accident, the sighting, and the disappearing. Everything beyond it is riddled with shadows, created by human imagination and the frantic yearning for closure.

Conspiracy theories may bloom in the shadows, but facts remain the anchor. They remind us of the boundaries of conjecture and of the obligation to respect the truth—even when it seems incomplete.

Perhaps the greatest lesson of Maura's disappearance is not that solutions are difficult, but that the quest for them shows the depths of human endurance. Families struggle for justice. Communities discuss, search, and question. Strangers commit themselves to keeping a name alive.

Maura Murray's narrative is unfinished—but it is not forgotten.

And maybe there is where the mystery continues to live: not just in the unsolved questions of what occurred on Route 112, but in the way her absence continues to demand presence in our collective memory.

Will the truth ever surface, or will it stay eternally out of reach—hidden in the solitude of that chilly New Hampshire night?

CLOSING SECTION

Key Lessons Learned

The disappearance of Maura Murray is more than a mystery trapped in time; it is a mirror exposing faults in justice, forensic science, and human perception. From this case, we find that the opening hours of an inquiry are frequently the most critical—yet also the most susceptible. Delays in coordinated response, contradictory witness testimony, and lost forensic chances may resonate for decades.

One of the harshest lessons is the requirement of transparent communication between law enforcement, families, and the public. Early doubt about what was known vs. what was assumed fostered the misunderstanding that exists today. It reminds us that transparency—without sacrificing investigative integrity—can avert years of guesswork.

On a personal level, Maura's abduction underlines the precarious balance between public curiosity and family anguish. Communities may mobilize to keep a case alive, but the weight of public preoccupation can also distort facts and create additional damage.

Ultimately, this case tells us that justice is not only about detecting crimes—it is about constructing mechanisms strong enough to resist ambiguity, prejudice, and the human urge to fill silence with supposition.

Modern Safety Strategies

While no preventative measure is infallible, readers today may benefit from the weaknesses this example showed. Safety is not merely about avoiding danger—it is about creating resilience in a contemporary, complicated society.

1. Physical Safety

Share the itinerary with trusted friends or family, particularly for trips into isolated places.

Invest in current technologies such as location-sharing apps or GPS-enabled emergency gadgets.

Trust your instincts: rejecting aid at a roadside may seem cautious, but balance that sense with prearranged emergency contacts who can arrive fast.

2. Digital Safety

Maintain awareness of how much personal information is exposed online. Offenders typically abuse overshared data such as habits, jobs, or vacation plans.

Use robust privacy settings and avoid displaying vulnerable moments—like flying alone—on social channels.

3. Psychological Awareness

Understand the persuasive strategies predators typically use: charm, urgency, phony authority, or feigned pity. Recognizing these patterns provides for better defenses.

Practice situational awareness: not paranoia, but the constant practice of examining surroundings and recognizing differences.

4. Community-Based Prevention

Advocate for better community alert systems. Neighbors and local witnesses are typically the first line of reaction, as Route 112 illustrated.

Build "safety circles": networks of friends, coworkers, or neighbors who check in periodically.

Safety now is not only about avoiding strangers—it is about equipping ourselves with tools, awareness, and networks that criminals cannot readily control.

Inside the Criminal Mind

Though Maura's destiny remains undetermined, researching perpetrators who abuse similar situations gives insight. Predators thrive in circumstances of turmoil and weakness. A stranded vehicle on a dark road, a lost visitor in a foreign town, or an individual navigating psychological turmoil—all present possibilities that criminals recognize.

Criminal psychology gives us three repeating traits:

- 1. Opportunism—Many predators are not master strategists. They wait for the unprotected time and attack when danger is low and vulnerability is high.
- 2. Manipulation—Successful criminals frequently use empathy as a weapon. They pitch themselves as helpers, abusing confidence before turning it against the victim.
- 3. Persistence—Predators rehearse mentally. They analyze patterns, perform little acts of duplicity, and test limits long before committing a significant crime.

By studying these patterns, we discover that criminals are not merely products of chance—they are patterned opportunists, sculpted by psychology, empowered by quiet, and successful because we typically underestimate them.

Honoring the Victims

It is tempting, in the maze of hypotheses and disputes, to lose sight of who Maura Murray genuinely was: a young woman with potential, complexity, and humanity. She was a daughter, a sister, a student, and a friend. Her life was not defined by a single event on Route 112, nor should she be remembered merely as a character in a mystery.

To celebrate Maura is to recall the fun she had with friends, the aspirations she set for her future, and the numerous tiny actions of everyday living that made her special. Every unresolved case is first and foremost a narrative of interrupted humanity.

For her family, the unsolved issues are not abstract riddles but experienced scars. Honoring Maura involves addressing not only the case but also the individuals who carry the silence every day.

Extended Resources

For those inspired by Maura's tale, support is not limited to curiosity. Here are worldwide resources for safety, missing individuals, and crisis intervention:

United States

National Center for Missing & Exploited Children (NCMEC): https://www.missingkids.org—Provides nationwide alerts, investigation help, and family aid.

RAINN (Rape, Abuse & Incest National Network): https://www.rainn.org—24/7 confidential help for survivors of sexual assault.

National Runaway Safeline: https://www.1800runaway.org — Support and services for runaway adolescents and families.

United Kingdom

Missing People UK: https://www.missingpeople.org.uk – Helpline and investigative help for missing individuals and families.

Victim Support UK: https://www.victimsupport.org.uk—Emotional and practical aid for victims of crime.

International

Interpol Yellow Notices: https://www.interpol.int—Assists in identifying missing individuals across borders.

International Centre for Missing & Exploited Children (ICMEC): https://www.icmec.org – Global advocacy, research, and training.

Each of these groups provides immediate, concrete help—from family therapy to cross-border investigation collaboration. For readers, sharing these resources may one day benefit another family in the quest for truth.

Final Reflection

The disappearance of Maura Murray is not merely a case—it is a disturbing reminder of how rapidly ordinary life may disintegrate. One moment she was driving, possibly with goals and intents known only to her; the next, she was gone.

The lesson is not to live in fear, but to live in awareness. To grasp that danger frequently lies in the everyday, that predators live in stillness, and that resilience is formed not by rejecting risk but by preparing for it.

Maura's tale will be carved in the collective memory of true crime, not because of its unresolved conclusion, but because it challenges us to consider uncomfortable questions about safety, justice, and how we memorialize people who disappear without answers.

In the end, the mystery of Route 112 is a mystery of mankind itself: frail, unexpected, and yet tenacious in its search for light.

And therefore the last, immovable truth is this: while Maura is absent, she is not forgotten. Her absence continues to resound as a cry for awareness, compassion, and justice—reminding us that even in quiet, tales deserve to be heard.

Printed in Dunstable, United Kingdom